JAI HANUMAN

Let's know about the story of Hanuman Ji. In the Assembly of Indra, the Lord of Gods, amongst a number of beautiful nymphs, one was named Punjiksthala. She was very restive and intemperate by nature. Once she disturbed a sage in his ... sage got annoyed and cursed her, "You have done an evil deed ... shall be born in the form of a she-monkey in your next birth." ... he fell at the feet of the sage and cried, "O sage! I beg your pard... knowingly. I did not mean to disturb your meditation or to insult ... ne and take back the curse."

Looking at Punjiksthala, the sage realized that Punjiksthala had really repented her actions and was sorry for her actions. So taking pity on her, the sage said, "I am sorry Punjiksthala the curse cannot be undone, but I can reduce it to the extent that you shall be able to change your form to that of a human being at your will." In due course of time, Punjiksthala was born to Kunjar who was one of the chiefs of monkeys. She was named Anjana.

Anjana was very beautiful as she had been in her earlier birth. When she grew up, she was married to another monkey-chief called Kesari. He was very strong and brave. When many years had passed, Kesari and Anjana got worried because no child had been born to them.

At last they prayed to Lord Shiva. They performed very hard penance. Shiva was pleased. He said, "You shall get a son who will he invincible. But for this, you have to seek the blessings of God Vayu, the Lord of Air.

Then Anjana started worshipping God Vayu. When the God was pleased, he appeared before her and said, "I am happy with your faith in me. Your wish will be granted. I, myself, shall be born to you. Thus your desire will be fulfilled." Kesari and Anjana were delighted that their wish was to be fulfilled and were going to get a son.

It is mentioned in many religious books that when he was born, he was wearing golden ear-rings. He had a cap on his head, which was decorated with rare jewels. Holy thread, Yagyopawit, was around his neck. The colour of his body, eyes and hair was golden yellow and a mace in one of his hands. He is also called the eleventh incarnation of Rudra, another incarnation of Shiva. Now, here is given the legend which relates how he came to be named 'Hanuman':

Once, while the son of Anjana was an infant, he was put in a cradle. She went out of the house on some errand. The child probably felt hungry or saw the sun in the sky and considered that to be a toy. He began to jump and leap up to get the sun. He, being the son of God Vayu, had immense energy. He leapt up and started flying into the sky. The God Vayu saw it and accompanied his son to protect him from the heat of the sun. He turned the hot air into a cool breeze.

Rahu, a demigod, was also heading towards the sun to eclipse him as that was a day of Amavasya. He saw the child going in the direction of the sun but did not pay any attention to him. When the son of the Vayu found Rahu within his reach, he pounced upon Rahu and grasped him in one of his hands.

Rahu was nonplussed. He did not know what to do. He was merely dumb founded. Having caught Rahu by the hair and head, Hanuman stood there fearlessly for some time. He stood cross- legged with the tip of his mace resting on the earth. Rahu exerted his full might to free himself from Hanuman's clutches.

The grip was very strong and with a great difficulty, Rahu freed himself and ran to Indra, the King of Gods, for rescue. He said, "O Lord of Gods! As commanded by you, when today I was going to eclipse the sun, another Rahu rushed to eat me up. It cannot be without your permission or order. Why have you put me in such a distress?"

Indra was nonplussed at what Rahu had said, "Who has the courage to eclipse the sun or eat Rahu?" He rode his divine elephant Airavat and rushed towards that child. Indra was frightened and shaken to find the child ready to attack him. He soon hurled the Vajra (Indra's heavelny weapon) or thunderbolt, and injured the flying Hanuman. 'Hanu' in Sanskrit means 'cheek'. This is how he came to be called "Hanuman".

Hanuman fell unconscious on the ground. His father, the God Vayu became very angry at Indra's act and withdrew from the atmosphere. He took Hanuman to a cave and greatly grieved. This resulted in the stoppage of air in the atmosphere. No living being could breathe. All the Gods, including Indra, led by Brahma, the Creator, appraoched God Vayu in the cave.

No one can live without air even for a moment. But as long as the air blows, nobody understands the importance of air. The moment it stops blowing, every creature feels suffocated.

Vayu lamented and explained to them what had happened. Brahma caressed Hanuman's body gently. He regained consciousness. His father's grief and anger subsided. Air began to blow again. Brahma granted Hanuman a boon that he would never be injured by any weapon. He asked other Gods also to bless Hanuman with divine powers. He said, "Bless him and he will always help you when none would stand by you." All the Gods granted him boons one by one.

Indra put a garland of heavenly flowers around Hanuman's neck and promised that in future Vajra would not affect him. The Sun God offered to educate him and granted him a portion of his brilliance. Kuber, the Lord of Yakshas, presented him with his mace. Shiva also granted him protection from his divine weapons. Brahma made him invincible and gave the power to change his form and size. He could go anywhere without any hindrance. Power to perform miracles too was bestowed upon him.

Thus Hanuman's adversity in his childhood became a blessing in disguise for him. He was armed with all the subtle and divine powers which made him unique and peerless.

Hanuman was a very restless and naughty boy. Great affection and protection, given to him by the Gods, spoilt him. He did not know what fear is. He played and fought with lions and elephants. He would never let the strong to bully the weak. He roamed about the hermitages of the sages and disturbed them in their meditation. He threw away their utensils and hung their seating mattresses on the high branches of trees. They complained to his parents who could not keep him under control.

At last a sage, in a fit of anger, cursed Hanuman, "O brave one! you are misusing your strength. As no other way is left, you shall not know the limit of your vigour and strength. Whenever needed you shall have to be invoke to do so. This is in the interest of yourself as well as others." Only God knows whether it was a curse or a boon. Hanuman was now very sober. Instead of teasing others, he began to help the sages in their daily chores. His parents and the hermits were very happy with him.

He had grown enough to begin his education. So his parents asked him to go to the Sun God to get his education.

His mother Anjana reminded him that he had as a child leapt into the sky to catch the sun. As soon as he was made to recall, he jumped high in the sky and flew away towards the sun. There he presented his salutations and said, "O Master! my name is Hanuman. I am Anjana's son. As directed by her, I submit myself to you to grant me all the knowledge I should possess."

The Sun God taught him Vedas, holy scriptures and other disciplines. Having learnt and absorbed all the teachings of his teacher, Hanuman prostrated before him and said, "My venerable teacher! By the grace of your blessings, I know the path of righteousness and duties meant for me. Now, what should I offer you in return what you deserve and desire?"

The Sun God replied, "Do one thing. Always take care of and protect Sugriva, the younger brother of Bali, thc monkey-king. He is born out of a portion of myself.

I foresee that very soon he is going to fall on very bad days and would need your help." Hanuman promised never to forget it and returned to his parents. His father advised him to go to Pampapur. This place was known as a centre of learning and traning in politics. There he came in contact with Sugriva. They became very intimate friends.

After the death of Bali, Sugriva became the king of Kishkindha. Bali and Sugriva were brothers. They loved each other very much. In the course of time, it so happend that they became arch enemies. Now, read this story:

Bali was the monkey king of Kishkindha, a son of Indra and the elder brohter of Sugriva. He was very strong and brave. His younger brother Sugriva treated him as his father. Bali was so powerful and valiant that demons, living near Kishkindha, never dared to enter his kingdom.

Once a demon, called Mayavee thought himself stronger than anyone. He came near Bali's palace and shouted, "O monkey-king! why are you hiding yourself? If you have the courage to face me, come out and fight with me. I shall teach you what bravery is."

Bali was annoyed at the way he was challenged by a demon. He decided to settle the score and came out of his palace to punish the demon for his insolence.

Sugriva also followed, since he feared for his brother. He wished to help his elder brother Bali. It was the dead of night. Sugriva knew that the power of a demon increases at night. Bali asked him to return to the palace, but Sugriva refused to leave. He thought he might come to the rescue of his elder brother in the hour of dire deed.

As soon as the demon saw Bali, he came to his senses and fled in fear. But Bali had made up his mind to kill him. To save himself from Bali's wrath, the demon entered into an aperture he found in the grounds. Bali saw him doing so and followed. But, before entering he turned to Sugriva and said, "I am going into this hole to chase the demon. Wait for me here. I shall be back after killing him. It may take some time. So, do not worry."

Saying this, Bali went inside the hole. As asked by his brother. Sugriva kept waiting for him for many days. When many weeks passed and Bali did not turn up, Sugriva got worried. He thought Bali had been killed by the demon. He put a rock at the mouth of the aperture so that the demon could not come out. He returned to Kishkindha dejected. When the ministers of Kishkindha saw Sugriva badly shaken and crest-fallen, they understood what had happened. They made Sugriva the king because Bali's son Angad was too young to rule the state. After sometime, Bali reappeared at Kishkindha after slaying the demon. When he found Sugriva was the king, shocked and agitated he came to the conclusion that his brother had deliberately put the rock to close the way out of the tunnel under the ground to cause his death.

Bali was in great rage. He said, "Ungrateful wretch! You thought you could kill me and steal the throne for yourself. You are a hundred times worse than Mayavi. I shall punish you and not let you live anymore."

Sugriva tried his best to explain and request his brother to calm down as he had never had such an idea. Bali did not listen to him. Sugriva was pained at Bali's behaviour whom he loved and respected very much. Bali turned him out of his kingdom and detained his wife as a punishment to Sugriva. He even rushed towards him to kill him. Sugriva knew well how strong Bali was. He ran away. Hanuman accompanied him. After having run for long, Sugriva and Hanuman entered the hermitage of sage Matanga. Bali had to stop there as he could not enter that place. Bali had been cursed once by the sage for some distespect, shown by Bali to him, that he would die the moment he touched the inside of his hermitage.

Sage Matanga lived at the Rishyamuk mountain. In this abode of that sage, Sugriva was safe. Though he was passing through very bad period, yet he had the good luck of Hanuman's friendship. Hanuman was a great help to him in organising a small group of welll-wishers.

Rama was in exile. Ravana, the demon king, had kidnapped Sita to Lanka. He with his brother Lakshman, was roaming in the forests in her search. When they reached Rishyamuk, Sugriva spotted them. He saw them armed with bows and arrows but wearing clothes of ascetics. The glow on their faces was heavenly and they looked very handsome, Sugriva could not make out whether they were warriors or sages, friends or foes. He thought, "May be they are agents or soldiers of Bali. He must have sent his demons in disguise to kill me." He was alarmed.

Sugriva expressed his fears to Hanuman. He himself went to see who those people were. He was very much impressed by the very appearance of Rama and Lakshman.

He was convinced that they could not be demons. He considered it better to have a talk with them. Then he approched them in the guise of a Brahman and spoke to them politely, "Who are you and where have you come from? What is the reason of your being here in the forest? You are wearing dress of ascetics but from appearance you are Kshatriyas. You are carrying weapons too. If I am not mistaken, you belong to some royal family. What makes you wander in such a dense and inhospitable forest? If I and my friends can be of any help to you, please do tell me."

Having listened to what Hanuman had said, Rama said to Lakshman, "This pious and handsome man, who stands before you, is certainly well-learned and intelligent. It is better for you to have a talk with him. This meeting may prove useful." Then Lakshman addressed Hanuman who was in the guise of a Brahman, "We both are sons of Dasharath, the King of Ayodhya. We are living in exile as ordered by him. He is my elder brother Rama. Ravana, the demon king, has kidnapped his wife Sita like a thief does. We are searching for her from place to place. This is the reason of our being here. Now, shall you please tell us who you are."

Hanuman was overwhelmed with emotions as soon as he learnt that he was face to face with Rama. He had been hearing about him since his childhood. He prostrated before Rama and said, "O my lord! I had forgotten that one day I must meet you as I am destined to serve you. I am at your disposal."

Hanuman forgot he was in disguise. He came out in his own self. Rama had recognised him. He picked him up and embraced him. After a few moments, Hanuman was normal. He said, "I am favoured. I am living here with my friend Sugriva. Because of some misunderstanding, his elder brother Bali is annoyed with him and bent upon killing him. He is very strong and brave but his mind has gone vile. He has kept Sugriva's wife in his possession causing great pain to him. Kindly help him. As soon as he gets back his wife and freedom from fear of Bali, he will give you all help he can. With your blessings, he will achieve both these. There is no doubt in it."

Rama promised to grant him freedom from fear. In the end, Bali was killed and Sugriva was made king of Kishkindha. Bali's widow Tara was too distressed to be consoled. On this occasion, Hanuman advised her not to wail over the death of her valiant husband. What Hanuman spoke ought to be read:

"Everyone, who is born, meets his fate according to his own deeds. These deeds result in pain and pleasure for all. Hence, one should keep one's mind under control so that the mind does not go astray. Nobody knows when the end would come. We must avoid committing sinful acts. He who follows the path of right thinking, does not lament or cry over the death of dear ones. One must look towards the future as the past is gone. One can better one's future only."

After Sugriva became king of Kishkindha, Bali's son Angad was made the Crown Prince. Hanuman was there to help Sugriva in administering the state. Sugriva was very happy. Rama was living in the forest. Lakshman desired that Sugriva should fulfil his promise of helping Rama in search for Sita. But he simply forgot that he owed to Rama what he had done for him. Rama was naturally worried.

Hanuman waited for some time to let Sugriva get settled. One day, when he could not wait anymore, he said to Sugriva, "You are now king of Kishkindha. The timely help of your friends and well-wishers has brought you this kingdom. You must be remembering what Rama has done for you. Therefore, it is the right time to help him in the fulfilment of his wish. He is expecting you to come forward and assist him in the search of his wife. You had promised to do so. Breach of trust does not behove you."

On the other hand, Rama was perturbed and waited for Sugriva's help. Lakshman was rather dejected at the plight of his elder brother. He was very furious. As he could bear no more, he souhgt Rama's permission to meet Sugriva. When he came to Kishkindha, everyone was alerted. Sugriva who had no time free from luxuries and enjoyments of life, was upset at the news of Lakshman's arrival. He said to Hanuman, "O son of Vayu! It is a very critical moment. Please pacify him as he is very angry. Also suggest to me what I can do in this matter. Rama is himself all powerful. How can I be of any use to him?"

Hanuman immediately arranged a meeting with Lakshman and said, "Kindly give up anger. King Sugriva can never think of breaking his promise. He is very much worried about Sita whom we consider as our mother. But he finds no way out. Please command us and we shall obey whatever you say. We shall leave no stone unturned to mitigate Lord Rama's agony."

After that, Sugriva, prince Angad and Hanuman accompanied by others, presented themselves before Rama. Sugriva bowed before him and begged his pardon for his default. Rama did not show any anger or malice towards Sugriva. He asked about his well-being. Sugriva said, "My Lord! be kind and excuse me. I, my friends and soldiers are ready to follow your orders as you please. Other monkey-chiefs too are present. In addition to this, anything else you wish will be available. We shall feel ourselves fortunate to be of any help to you."

Rama said, "O King of Kishkindha! I think you know that my main worry at this time is to find where and how Sita is. How it can be done may be decided by you and your friends." Sugriva there and then assigned the task of finding out the whereabouts of Sita to the monkeys and the bears. Then he said to Hanuman, "You can approach all the worlds, the seas, the earth and the sky without any hindrance. Therefore, I request you to find out where Sita is. It is not difficult for you."

Taking leave of Rama, Hanuman said, "My Lord! By your grace, I shall come back with the desired information. Give me your ring as a token of identity."

Hanuman, the embodiment of strength and greatness, along with his companions, was passing through the forests and mountains, when the monkeys and the bears reached a place where they found no water or food for many days. They began to fall sick and were tired. Then suddenly, they saw a cave. They entered it and at its other end, they found trees bearing fruits and spings of fresh water. They could not resist themselves. In that beautiful garden, a very beautiful woman was meditating under a tree. Her concentration was disturbed. When she opened her eyes, she found her garden being destroyed. She was very much annoyed. She asked them to stop, "What are you doing? You are damaging this heaven-like place." Hanuman replied with great humility, "O honourable maiden! Please forgive us. Afflicted by hunger and thirst, these friends of mine could not control themselves. We are searching for Sita, my Lord's wife who has been kidnapped by a demon. But what are you doing here where we see not a single soul?"

That beautiful young lady was Swyamprabha, daughter of a Gandharva. She said, "Oh! you are a devotee of Lord Rama who is an incarnation of Lord Vishnu, the Preserver! It is my good fortune that you happen to come here. My austere worship is over. I was waiting for his arrival in these forests as the piety of his feet would grant me salvation and a place in the heaven. You shall succeed in your mission, there can be no dobut about it. How can devotees of Rama face failure?"

Under the leadership of Hanuman, the armies of monkeys and bears reached the sea from the forests. From there they could not proceed further. All of them were in a fix as to what to do. They could not go back without any news about Sita. They were pained and demoralised. Sugriva would not even hear the word 'failure'. They would surely be condemned to death. And, what would Rama think of them? They decided to die themselves by not taking any food and water. They did not have the courage to face Rama or Sugriva. They wished they were of any use to their Lord as the vulture-king Jatayu had done. They were not as fortunate as he was to give up their lives in the cause of Lord Rama.

On the beach of the sea, in the Vindhya mountain nearby, a brother of great Jayayu lived in a cave. His name was Sampati. Sampati was disturbed by the great noise created by the wailing monkeys and the bears. He came out of the cave. At the sight of a large army of monkeys and bears crying for death, he was very pleased. He thought he would get food for a long period. But when he heard the name of his brother being mentioned by them, he was alarmed. He came near the monkeys and said to them, "Brave monkeys! Just now you were talking of Jatayu. He is my brother. I have not seen him for many years. What were you saying about him? Kindly tell me what that was."

The monkeys were scared to see an unbelievably large vulture. They were however encouraged to talk to him when they found that he had no feathers and was thus harmless.

The monkeys told Sampati that Jatayu died while fighting against Ravana when he was kidnapping Sita.

Sampati was grief-stricken at the sad news of his brother’s death. He prayed to the monkeys to take him to the beach so that he might offer water to his departed brother's soul.

Hanuman lifted Sampati and put him on the head of the sea. After having offered water to his brother Jatayu’s soul, he prayed to God for his salvation. When he was composed, he said, “I can see that on the other side of the sea, there is a city. Yes, that is the city of Lanka. Name of this city’s king is Ravan. He is very powerful and a great devotee of Lord Shiva.”

“He is so strong and valiant that even Gods tremble before him. In one of his garden, a goddess-like woman is sitting under a tree in very pensive mood and miserable state. She must be Sita. Friends, I am unable to offer you any physical help. This is what I could do for you.”

All the monkeys and the bears discussed what should be done. Crossing of the sea was not possible. Having known the place where Sita was put was of no use to them. They were helpless. Being the most experienced and senior person, Jambavant was expected to guide them. He looked towards Hanuman and said, "Why are you silent? Can one believe that Rama's desire

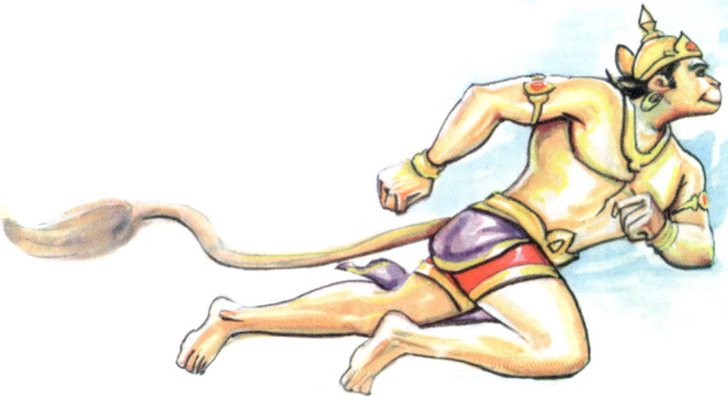

may remain unfulfilled? True, none of us can cross the sea. But O greatest of all! you are the son of God Vayu. Crossing the sea by flying should not be a difficult job for you. Recall that you caught and grasped Rahu in one jump only. Raise your power. This is the time to put an end to Rama's anxiety by coming to your own."

Jambavant invoked Hanuman's latent powers. His face was full of divine glow. He enlarged his body and said, "I, the son of Vayu, am willing and ready to go to do any duty as desired by my Lord Rama. Tell me what I should do. May I burn Lanka of Ravan and bring Sita back on my shoulders or may I present the demon as a captive at his feet? Or, should I bring the news and welfare of Sita only? The sea cannot be an obstruction in my way. Say and I shall empty it of its waters or drive it deep into the earth. Just tell me what is expected of me."

Jambavant was now satisfied with his form and confidence. He said, "O the son of Anjana! you are great and you are invincible. You are all mighty. No doubt, you can tear apart the earth and find the place where Sita is and how she is."

With the name of Rama on his lips, Hanuman jumped up to fly away. When he jumped to the sky both the earth and the sky were shaken. The Gods in the heaven were alarmed at his roar. With the blessings of his father, the speed of his flight appeared to be piercing the sky.

The Gods were apprehensive of the extent of Hanuman’s strength. To test his intelligence and valour, they asked Surasa, the mother of cobras, to change herself into a ferocious rakshas woman and obstruct his progress. She agreed and transformed herself into an enormous rakshas woman and placed herself in Hanuman's route as he continued to rush across the sea. Sursa roared, “Beware! you cannot go any further. I am hungry and shall satisfy my hunger by devouring you.” Hearing what Surasa demanded, Hanuman replied, “O mother! kindly accept my greetings and respectful salutations. I am in a hurry as I am on a mission. I promise that I shall offer myself to you once I am free. Then, you may eat me with pleasure. But, please let me go now.”

Surasa did not listen to Hanuman’s pleas. To test the wit and grit of Hanuman, she said, “Lord Brahma has decreed that I will get to eat everything and everyone that comes near me. Let me see if you have it in you to enter my mouth and still come out alive.”

Hanuman entered Sursa's mouth and enlarged his size. Sursa too expanded her mouth. This was what Hanuman had been waiting for. In an instant, he shrank back to his normal size and jumped out of Sursa's huge mouth. Sursa was pleased by Hanuman's intelligence. She blessed him and said, “Success by yours.”

Having crossed the sea, Hanuman reached Trikut mountain where Ravana's Lanka was situated. He found that Lanka was a very beautiful city. Protected from all sides by high walls, it was very difficult to enter the city. It was surrounded by the ocean. Below, in the city, he saw great hustle and bustle everywhere. It was so well-decorated and full of grand mansions and houses that even palaces in the heaven were no match to them. Well-armed soldiers were protecting the streets. Hanuman thought that during night he might be able to get entry into Lanka. War with Ravana seemed to be definite. Therefore, every aspect should be looked into. Any lapse or flaw in preparation would prove disastrous.

Nothing could be left to chance or risk. Hence, in the darkness of night, he entered Lanka by slipping into it having diminshed his size.

During his search for Sita's place of captivity, he noted with care the quality of the weapons of Ravan's soldiers, the stables of horses and elephants and his armoury. He also noticed that there were many demons who were good at heart and God-fearing. But there was no trace of Sita anywhere. He was worried and surprised as to where he had kept her. At last, he jumped into Ravana's palace. In the open space, around the palace within the four walls he saw even flying machines. In the nearby houses and quarters many young and beautiful women were visible but Sita was not among them.

Hanuman came out of Ravana's palace with great disappointment. While walking around, he suddenly saw a temple. He was amazed to find it in the city of demons. The day was about to break. Hanuman went inside the temple. There in the temple a saintly person was worshipping Lord Rama. He was reciting Lord Rama's name. Hanuman presented himself in the guise of a Brahman before that person when he had performed all his religious rituals. Hanuman wished him with "Rama-Rama". He was very much astonished. He was as well pleased to meet a devotee of Rama. That man was none else but Vibhishan, younger brother of Ravana. Vibhishan, a devotee of Rama, was immensely pleased to meet Hanuman, another devotee of Rama.

Vibhishan inquired who Hanuman was and how a God-worshipper could be found in Lanka. Hanuman told him everything and the aim of his being there.

Vibhishan told Hanuman that he would find Sita sitting under the Ashoka tree near Ravana's palace.

Leaving Vibhishan in the temple. Hanuman returned to Ravana's palace. It took him no time to locate the Ashoka tree. He saw Sita in very low spirits and a miserable state as described by Vibhishan. All of a sudden, the she-demons became alert as their was a great noise of drum-beating and running of horses. Hanuman concealed himself in the branches and leaves of the tree he was sitting in.

That was the signal of Ravana's arrival in the garden. He came straight to Sita and said, "I have come again to make you understand that you should agree to my proposal. This is the only way left for you."

When Ravana had finished, Sita said, "You are a demon and shall always remain a demon. You are not aware of what is going to happen. You are doomed to die at Lord Rama's hand soon."

Ravana was furious at Sita's bitter rebukes to him. He once again ordered the demon guards to bring her round by hook or by crook. Then he left the place.

When Sita was left alone, she began to cry bitterly. Hanuman could not wait anymore. He spoke from within the hiding place up in the tree, "Mother! I am Hanuman and have come to you as a messenger of Lord Rama."

As soon as Sita heard Rama's name, her face bloomed like a flower of morning. Hanuman jumped down. When Sita saw him, she was perplexed.

Hanuman at once understood what in Sita's mind was. He was sure that Sita did not believe him.

Then he increased his body. Sita had no doubt anymore that Hanuman was not a demon and had been sent by Rama. She was happy. Hanuman said to her, "This is the ring my Lord has given me to show to you so that you are consoled." Hanuman assured Sita that Lord Rama would soon kill Ravana.

Sita's joy knew no bounds at what Hanuman had said. She said to Hanuman, "You are a true devotee of Rama. Tell him that he should come and save me from the demon. So far as these trees are concerned, they belong to Ravan. Very strong and armed demons are there to guard these trees. Take care of yourself. Rama will protect you from all evils. Now, enjoy these fruits to your heart's content."

Taking Sita's permission, Hanuman climbed up a tree and began to eat fruits of many trees. He ate the ripe and sweet fruits but threw away the raw ones. When his hunger was satisfied, an idea came to his mind, "Should I not let these guards around the Ashoka tree and the rest of the demons know that it can be trespassed. This will also show how brave and alert these soldiers are." Thus, he started destroying the trees and plants which were carefully looked after. When the garden was ravaged, there was great confusion amongst the demon guards. Hanuman jumped up the rampart of Ravana's palace.

Hanuman raised such a storm that the guards and soldiers could do nothing and were helpless before an ordinary monkey. They together rushed towards him but they could not even touch him. Then, they took their swords out of their sheaths and threw their spears towards him. Hanuman's hands and tail were so fast that he not only saved himself from the attack but gave them a good thrashing too. The she-demons came running to Sita lest she should be harmed or taken away by the monkey. The demons came running to Ravana and told him what had happened.

Ravana could not believe them and shouted, "What are you saying? A monkey has destroyed the Ashoka garden which even Gods dare not enter! How can anyone have the courage and the guts to sneak into my palace?" The demons said, "Our Lord! This is not the case. We tried our best to catch him but he jumps and bounces like a ball from one tree to another. Our weapons have proved useless. Have a look at us. He is responsible for this plight of ours."

Ravana ordered one of his army commanders to present Hanuman before him at once. The army commander took his soldiers with him to the high wall of the palace where Hanuman was destroying whatever he found. The demon soldiers shot arrows at Hanuman. At that stage, Hanuman was enjoying the action. He could not even be injured. On the other hand, the army commander was killed with a single assault of Hanuman's mace. The soldiers took to their heels. Then many more demon warriors were sent to arrest him. They all lost their lives.

When Hanuman could not be apprehended, Ravana asked his younger son Akshaya to do the needful. Akshaya climbed his cahriot and reached the scene of fight between Hanuman and the demons. He was fully armed and protected by his army. Hanuman wanted to make clear to Ravana what Rama's devotee could do and what strength or power he possessed. When Akshaya attacked, Hanuman retaliated. Akshaya's chariot was destroyed and his charioteer was killed. Akshaya drew his sword and made an assault on Hanuman. Hanuman jumped up in the sky. Akshaya tried to jump and tried to brandish his sword. In turn, Hanuman caught hold of his leg and revolved him in the air. Akshaya fell dead on the ground.

Ravana was greatly shocked at the news of his son's death. He was so enraged that he decided to punish Hanuman himself. Then his elder son Meghanad said, "O father! I shall punish the killer of Akshaya. You need not take this trouble. There is no question of your going to catch a monkey while I am here."

Saying so, he rode his cahriot and rushed to capture Hanuman. Meghanad attacked fiercely by showering arrows. Hanuman was injured and blood began to flow out. This annoyed him. He pulled up a very huge iron pillar from the ground and threw towards Meghanad. Meghanad saved his life by jumping out of his chariot. But his chariot and a number of accompanying soldiers were smashed.

When Meghanad's weapons could not harm Hanuman, he threw lariat which had been given to him by Brahma. Hanuman had the power to free himself yet he did not do so. It would have been an insult to Brahma, the Creator. Moreover, he wanted to return to Rama soon. He let Meghanad arrest him. He was tied with a very thick and strong rope so that he could not escape. As soon as he was tied with the rope, the divine lariat freed him. He did nothing. That was the right time to have a look at Ravana and warn him. Meghanad took Hanuman to Ravana's court.

Hanuman was absolutely fearless. He was not at all afraid of Ravana or his great courtiers. The glamour of Ravana's court did not have any adverse impact on him.

The minister and army commanders, at Ravana's court, were stunned when they saw Hanuman. They failed to understand who that monkey could be and how he had routed an army of demons. One of the ministers asked Hanuman, "O monkey! Who are you and where have you come from? Why have you entered Lanka or have you been asked by someone else? If you speak the truth, you may be pardoned."

Hanuman looked around and spoke to Ravana, "O King of Lanka! I am called Hanuman and am a companion of Sugriva, the King of Kishkindha. I am a humble servant of Lord Rama. I am here as his messenger. You have kidnapped his wife Sita."

Ravana could listen no more. He was agitated and ordered angrily, that Hanuman should be killed. Hanuman did not react.

All the soldiers, present in the court of Ravana, rushed towards Hanuman. Ravana's younger brother Vibhishan intervened and said, "Wait, this monkey has come here in the capacity of an emissary. He had brought a message from Rama. You are well aware of the fact that slaying of an emissary is prohibited. If he deserves a punishment, do punish him but you must not kill him". Ravana accepted Vibhishan's plea and ordered Hanuman's tail to be set on fire because a monkey loves his tail most of all. It was the maximum Ravana could do.

The demons wrapped Hanuman's tail with rags and doused in oil before lighting it. Hanuman jumped high and began to burn Ravana's palace. The palace was soon in flames like a house of wax. The adjacent buildings too caught fire. Everyone was in panic. Nobody had the time even to look towards the roayal palace. The stalls and the arm stores were reduced to ashes. People began to assemble in open spaces. There was a great turmoil. When Hanuman was satisfied at the punishment he had given Ravana, he went to Sita and took her leave. He put out the fire on his tail in the sea and flew back to where the army of monkeys and bears was waiting anxiously for him.

It must be noted very carefully and tenderly that the entire Lanka was reduced to ashes by Hanuman, but Vibhishan's house was untouched. How could a devotee of Lord Rama be hurt! Hanuman himself was not burnt by the fire because he happened to be the ambassador of the Lord who created fire itself, So Hanuman himself along with Vibhishan and his family were untouched by fire! They alone were safe and sound!

The good news of Hanuman's success in locating Sita was welcomed with great applause and pleasure. Jambavant blessed Hanuman. From there, all of them marched to Rama's place. When Sugriva saw them jumping and dancing, he knew that Hanuman had the good news about Sita. Hanuman told Rama all that had happened. Rama said, "Dear Sugriva! Now, we should set out to Lanka. You may order your friends and soldiers to get ready."

Sugriva, Jambavant and other chieftains led their armies to the sea-shore. Nala and Neel, the great architects built bridge over the sea with the help of brave monkeys and bears. Ultimately they crossed the sea and camped in the vicinity of Lanka.

You have read Rama-Ravana war in the "Ramayana" in detail. Hanuman had the power to perform miracles as has been told in earlier pages of this book. Here is another example of his power. Lakshman fell into a swoon when he was struck with a 'Shakti' by Meghnath.

Everyone was depressed. Jambavant again invoked Hanuman to fly to the Himalayas. He reminded Hanuman that none but he had the power and strength to bring the Sanjivani herb in time! Hanuman flew to the Himalayas clearing all hurdles on the way. There he saw different kinds of herbs. He could not recognize the Sanjivani herb. So Hanuman lifted up the entire hill. He brought the life-giving herb well in time. The herb was immediately applied on Lakshman's wounds. His swoon was soon over. Thus Hanuman proved to be the saviour of Lakshman. Everybody was grateful to him.

There was wailing and weeping in every house in Lanka as countless demons had been killed.

After Meghnath and Khumbhkaran had been killed Ravana himself came to the battle-field to fight against Rama.

Ravana mounted on his golden chariot shot a spate of arrows at Rama. The two supreme bowmen were bent upon slaying each other. They shot potent missiles of secret power. The Gods in heaven looked on with wonder and admiration.

Rama pierced with his arrows every limb of Ravana, yet he did not fall. Matali, Rama's Charioteer, reminded him to use Brahma-astra. Having uttered the spell, Rama shot the Brahma astra which pierced Ravana's chest where was enshrined the secret of his invincibility. The nectar in his naval was dried up. Ravana fell down dead from his chariot to the battle-field.

The Gods in heaven blew their trumpets and showered flowers!